Prisoners of The Blob

Prisoners of The Blob

Why most education experts are wrong about nearly everything

Toby Young

Civitas: Institute for the Study of Civil Society
London

First Published April 2014

© Civitas 2014
55 Tufton Street
London SW1P 3QL

email: books@civitas.org.uk

ISBN 978-1-906837-61-7

Independence: Civitas: Institute for the Study of Civil Society is a registered educational charity (No. 1085494) and a company limited by guarantee (No. 04023541). Civitas is financed from a variety of private sources to avoid over-reliance on any single or small group of donors.

All publications are independently refereed. All the Institute's publications seek to further its objective of promoting the advancement of learning. The views expressed are those of the authors, not of the Institute.

Typeset by
Civitas

Printed in Great Britain by
Berforts Group Ltd
Stevenage SG1 2BH

Contents

Author

Toby Young is the co-founder of the West London Free School, the first free school to sign a funding agreement with Michael Gove. He is the author of three books, *How to Lose Friends and Alienate People* (2001), *The Sound of No Hands Clapping* (2006) and *How to Set Up a Free School* (2011), and an associate editor of *The Spectator*. His teaching experience includes working as a teaching fellow at Harvard and a teaching assistant at Cambridge. He is currently a visiting fellow at the University of Buckingham and a Fulbright Commissioner.

Prisoners of The Blob

Why most education experts are wrong about nearly everything

Introduction

What is The Blob and what has a 1950s sci-fi movie got to do with education policy? Michael Gove, the Secretary of State for Education, uses it as a catch-all term to describe the opponents of education reform, but he's thinking in particular of the leaders of the teaching unions, local authority officials, academic experts and university education departments.[1] In this, he's following the lead of William J. Bennett, the former US Education Secretary, who originally coined the term to describe the army of educationalists, lobbyists and government officials who obstructed his attempts to reform America's public education system in the 1980s. He used it specifically to refer to the 'bloated educational bureaucracy'.

It's a good term, and not just because it conveys the sheer scale of the opposition reformers like Gove and Bennett face. (In the film the amoeba-like alien threatens to consume an entire town.) It also captures the ability of the educational establishment to withstand attack, becoming stronger each time an opponent is absorbed into the amorphous mass. Witness the failure of Bennett's attempts to reform America's public education system and the failure of successive governments, both Labour and Conservative, to reverse the decline of Britain's state schools. As the former Education Minister George Walden wrote in the *Telegraph*: 'Reforming education, a friend sighed on my appointment, was like trying to disperse a fog with a hand grenade: after the flash and the explosion, the fog creeps back. So it proved under Thatcher, and so it has been under Blair and Brown.'[2] Even when key positions in the education-industrial complex are captured by members of the pro-reform camp, like Chris Woodhead, who became the head of Ofsted in 1994, it makes little impression. 'My single biggest doubt about Ofsted stems from the fact that some inspectors are unwilling or unable to jettison their progressive educational views,' he wrote in *Class War* (2002).[3]

But this way of looking at The Blob – as professionals who have a vested interest in preserving the status quo, the 'producer interest' – is slightly misleading. What's remarkable about the educational establishment, both here and in America, is the fact that nearly everyone in it shares the same progressive educational philosophy. They all believe that skills like 'problem-solving' and 'critical thinking' are more important than subject knowledge; that education should be 'child-centred' rather than 'didactic' or 'teacher-led'; that 'group work' and 'independent learning' are superior to 'direct instruction'; that the way to interest children in a subject is to make it 'relevant'; that 'rote-learning' and 'regurgitating facts' is bad, along with discipline, hierarchy, routine and anything else that involves treating the teacher as an authority figure. The list goes on. Their adherence to this ideology is so fanatical that they ignore the huge body of empirical evidence that shows progressive teaching methods don't work, as well as the findings of cognitive scientists. After three decades of research, cognitive scientists have concluded that abilities like critical thinking and problem solving cannot be taught to children as stand-alone, abstract 'skills'. They can only be taught alongside subject knowledge.

The resistance to the reforms proposed by Michael Gove and William Bennett isn't self-interested, at least not primarily. The reason the leaders of the education-industrial complex are so hostile is because the traditional approach to education favoured by these conservative politicians – that first and foremost it should be about the transmission of knowledge – is at odds with theirs. A case in point is the letter 100 academics wrote to the *Telegraph* on 20 March 2013, opposing Gove's curriculum reforms. 'The proposed curriculum consists of endless lists of spellings, facts and rules,' they complained. 'This mountain of data will not develop children's ability to think, including problem-solving, critical understanding and creativity.'[4]

Members of The Blob shouldn't be thought of as bureaucrats fighting to defend their little patch. Rather, they're evangelists for a quasi-religious cause, soldiers in a secular crusade that dates back to the Romantic Movement. Often, they don't realise they've been enlisted in this campaign. They imagine that their educational ideas are just plain common sense, backed up by empirical evidence. *Of course it's a bad idea for children to learn Latin verbs – and here's the 'research' to prove it!* In this respect, they're less like the red blancmange in *The Blob* and more like the innocent townsfolk who've been enslaved by the aliens in *Invasion of the Body Snatchers.*

I prefer to think of The Blob as a particular ideological outlook rather than the people who've been captured by it. It's a creed, a movement – what the American educationalist E.D. Hirsch calls a 'thoughtworld'. For those of us who favour a knowledge-building, teacher-led approach, it is this ideology that is the enemy, not those who believe in it. For the most part, they are well-intentioned, well-meaning people who share the same goals we do. Like us, they want to devise a public education system that helps all children lead rich and fulfilling lives, no matter what their background. They also share our desire to reduce the attainment gap between children from low-income families and their high-income peers. It's just that they are misguided – imprisoned by a 200-year-old belief system – as I hope to show in what follows.

The Thoughtworld

The central pillar of The Blob's educational philosophy is the belief that children are essentially good. That is, children are naturally curious, imaginative and creative and the purpose of a good education is to enable children to express fully these innate talents. That means not starting children's formal education too early; an emphasis on learning through doing rather than direct instruction or repetition; and as few facts as possible. Education should be child-centred, starting from what's already familiar – pop music, TV shows, video games – and building up from there. A good school should cultivate every aspect of a child's nature, not just his or her ability to memorise names and dates or use reason and logic. Instead of trying to suppress children's more unruly characteristics, teachers should focus on 'the whole being'.

As we shall see, many of these ideas can be traced back to the Romantic Movement, but they've gained additional authority in the last half-century or so from the rise of post-modernism and, in particular, from the belief that what we think of as knowledge, including scientific knowledge, is just one way of looking at the world, with no greater claim to being true than any other. In the

British and American university departments where prospective teachers learn their trade, this epistemological relativism has become the orthodoxy. Indeed, a general scepticism about the value of knowledge – particularly traditional subject knowledge – is so ubiquitous that the old-fashioned approach to education that still prevails in Catholic schools, selective state schools and high-performing private schools has almost no defenders. Knowing the names of the Kings and Queens of England is dismissed as 'rote-learning of facts from the national patriotic narrative'[5] and of no relevance to children born into a modern, multi-cultural society like ours. It's only one 'perspective' in a complex story – a 'middle-class' perspective, in the words of Professor John White of the Institute of Education, Britain's leading teaching training college.[6] According to the post-modernist Gospel, all knowledge is 'socially constructed' and no one point of view is more valid than any another.[7]

Some progressive 'thought leaders' even believe this applies to mathematics. Jo Boaler, a professor at Stanford, has coined the term 'ethnomathematics' to convey just how 'bourgeois' and 'white' maths is. According to one exasperated reformer, Boaler believes that 'traditional mathematics – the mathematics taught in universities around the world – is the property of Western Civilisation and is inexorably linked with the values of the oppressors and conquerors'.[8]

Professors of education like Boaler think that instead of transmitting 'ethnocentric' knowledge, the job of the teacher – or rather 'learning facilitator' – is to furnish children with the 'skills and competencies' they'll need to get jobs in our fast-moving, global economy, as well as turning them into 'responsible citizens'. They're not supposed to learn anything in the boring, old-fashioned sense of the word, e.g. commit facts to memory. Rather, they should learn how to learn – or 'learn 2 learn'. This involves 'cross-curricula work' in which 'learners' (never pupils) are taught about 'concepts' and 'themes' through a multiplicity of different 'lenses'. Any suggestion of a hierarchical relationship between teacher and student, such as the notion that teachers might actually know something that their pupils don't, is completely taboo. The aim of a good teacher is to be a 'guide on the side' rather than a 'sage on the stage'. (As you'd expect from a quasi-religious movement, The Blob's thoughtworld is full of these rhyming mantras. Other terms for dismissing the teaching of knowledge include 'drill and kill' and 'chalk and talk'.)

History – Or, Rather, 'Detecting Bias' and 'Role Play'

This progressive approach, while it has its roots in a movement that dates back to the eighteenth century, has only become ubiquitous in the public education systems of Britain and America comparatively recently. To illustrate its shortcomings, let's look at the way history is currently taught in English schools. When I studied A-level history in the early 1980s at William Ellis, a grammar school in North London, the approach to the subject hadn't changed much since Edward Gibbon. It was simple and straightforward: you studied the great events of the past and understood them as part of an over-arching chronological narrative.[9] Not today. Rather than teaching children about the past, the job of the history teacher is to furnish them with the skills of a professional historian. Not so much history as historiography.

In a typical lesson, the teacher presents pupils with a primary source – an extract from the diary of Cecil

Rhodes, for instance – and invites them to 'detect bias', i.e. circle those words and phrases that from our vantage point in the twenty-first century are unacceptably racist or sexist. In this way, history ceases to be about teaching children some perspective so they can transcend the tyranny of the present. Instead, it becomes a tool for reinforcing it. This is what prompted Robert Tombs, a professor of history at Cambridge, to describe the skills-based approach as 'crassly present-centred' and 'vapidly self-congratulatory'.[10]

Detecting bias is the main stock-in-trade of professional historians, apparently, but children are also taught other techniques for convincing themselves just how noble and wise they are compared to their backward forebears. No history lesson is complete without at least 15 minutes of 'role play' in which learners pretend to be the victim of some past social injustice. Here's an actual example from a website called 'activehistory.co.uk', a commonly used resource by history teachers in England's secondary schools:

> Take on the role of a kidnapped young African and see how well you can maintain your strength in the harrowing 'Middle Passage' across the Atlantic in this decision-making activity. Complete with five different lesson plans.

Here's another example, this one singled out by Ofsted as an example of 'good practice':

> The teachers ensured that the pupils had experiences to help them formulate ideas and give a context to and content for their writing. For example, Year 3/4 pupils spent an hour on the school field, trying out hoeing, digging and bird-scaring before recounting the life of a Victorian child as a farm labourer.[11]

Whatever else children might be learning while performing these exercises, they aren't learning history. They aren't being asked to think about history – which they can't because they aren't being taught any historical knowledge – but about themselves.

This way of teaching history is supposed to be 'value-free', yet a cursory glance at any of the accompanying materials quickly puts paid to that myth. According to Christopher McGovern, the Chairman of the Campaign for Real Education who has taught history to 5-18 year-olds for over 30 years, the 'obsession with political correctness' in this approach is clear. 'If a battle is taught it is as likely to be through a "social" or "gender" perspective – conditions on board HMS Victory or the role of women in World War I munitions factories – than it is to be about military events at Trafalgar or El Alamein.'[12]

McGovern goes on to describe the contents of a standard GCSE history textbook called *Minds and Machines* (1999):

> Traditional heroes including Clive of India, General Wolfe, Admiral Nelson, Florence Nightingale and General Gordon are all excluded from this national curriculum textbook on the period 1750 to 1900. The Duke of Wellington's role in history is confined to his opposition to the Chartists. There is no mention of his role at Waterloo: the book promotes Peterloo, not Waterloo.[13]

McGovern isn't the only history teacher to have reservations about the progressive approach. His views are echoed by Robert Peal, a young teacher who cut his teeth at a comprehensive in Birmingham:

> It did not take me long to work out why pupils are so ignorant of British history, despite spending over a year studying it (as laid down by the national curriculum). To

study the Norman Conquest, pupils would re-enact the Battle of Hastings in the playground, conduct a classroom survey to create their own Domesday Book, and make motte-and-bailey castles out of cereal boxes. Medieval England would be studied through acting out the death of Thomas Becket and creating a board game to cover life as a medieval peasant. For the Industrial Revolution, pupils pitched inventions to Dragons' Den and lessons on the British Empire culminated in the design of a commemorative plate showing whether it was or was not a 'force for good'.[14]

The upshot of this Blue Peter approach to teaching history is that children leave school knowing next to nothing about the past. The Conservative peer Lord Ashcroft commissioned a survey in the summer of 2012 that revealed more children associate the name 'Churchill' with the animated dog in the car insurance adverts than with Britain's war-time prime minister. And such ignorance is far from exceptional. Here's McGovern again, this time discussing the results of a survey commissioned by the BBC in 2004 to test people's knowledge of landmark events:

Half of the younger age group [16-24 year-olds] did not know the Battle of Britain happened during World War II and almost a half could not connect Sir Francis Drake to the battle against the Spanish Armada, naming, instead, Gandalf, Horatio Hornblower or Christopher Columbus. Seventy-one per cent of over-65s know that the famous battle marked every year on 12th July by the Orangemen in Northern Ireland is the Battle of the Boyne. In contrast, this was known by only 18 per cent of 16-24 year-olds. Fifteen per cent of these youngsters thought the Orangemen were celebrating victory at Helms Deep, the fictional battle in Tolkien's *Lord of the Rings*. A survey in 2003 revealed that 30 per cent of 11-18 year-olds thought that Oliver Cromwell fought at the Battle of Hastings and a similar number could not name the century for the First World War. Fewer than half of the 200 children questioned knew that Nelson's flagship at Trafalgar was the Victory. Similarly, a Channel 4 poll on the history of the monarchy, commissioned to accompany the David Starkey series on the topic, found that only one in 10 young people could connect King John to Magna Carta. At the extreme end we read of some youngsters who think Adolf Hitler was Britain's prime minister during World War II and that the Roman occupation happened a mere 150 years ago.[15]

The same progressive approach to teaching history prevails in America's public school system and, not surprisingly, American schoolchildren are as ignorant of their own past as ours are. In *What Do Our 17-Year-Olds Know?* (1987), Diane Ravitch and Chester Finn reveal that 43 per cent of high school seniors can't place World War One between 1900 and 1950, more than two-thirds of them cannot name the half-century in which the Civil War took place and more than 75 per cent are unable to say within 20 years when Abraham Lincoln was President.[16]

William Bennett is equally despairing about American schools in *Devaluing America* (1992), his memoir about his tenure as Education Secretary:

> According to the NAEP-based survey of 21-to-25-year-olds conducted in 1986, fewer than 40 per cent were able to interpret an article by a newspaper columnist. And the situation is worse among minorities: just one in 10 black young adults and two in 10 Hispanic young adults can satisfactorily interpret the same newspaper column. In 1989, *National Geographic* did a survey of geography knowledge. Americans aged 18 to 24 finished last among 10 countries, including Mexico.[17]

Ian Livingstone CBE

In light of all the evidence about how ineffective progressive teaching methods are, you'd think they'd have been abandoned by now. But no. Every time a progressive theory is discredited, it resurfaces under a new name and masquerades as an 'innovation'. This explains why there are so many different labels for child-centred education – 'independent learning', 'incidental learning', 'discovery learning', 'project-based learning', etc.[18] One of the most striking characteristics of The Blob – both in the sci-fi film and in the educational sense – is its ability to regenerate. For every educationalist that sees the light and recognises the importance of knowledge, another springs up in his place, spouting the same old jargon – or 'eduspeak', as it's sometimes known. The Blob has an extraordinary facility for capturing people, for turning them into mouthpieces for its progressive educational ideas.

Take Ian Livingstone CBE, one of the founders of the UK games industry. He recently gave an interview to *The Times* in which he announced he was setting up a free school in London embodying an approach that he clearly thought of as radical and new – something that had never been tried before.

According to the article, Livingstone believes children should 'learn through play' rather than be subjected to 'Victorian' rote-learning. In this way, they'll discover how to 'solve problems' and be 'creative', instead of being forced to memorise 'irrelevant' facts that can be accessed 'at the click of a mouse'. He dismissed exams as 'random memory tests' that have 'far more to do with league tables than learning'.[19]

In saying all this, Livingstone didn't seem to be aware that he was parroting The Blob's standard criticism of the old-fashioned, 'chalk and talk' model in which children are asked to commit facts to their long-term memories.

Richard Evans, the regius professor of modern history at Cambridge, made a similar point recently about the new history curriculum – and no doubt he, too, doesn't realise he's an intellectual prisoner of The Blob. History, he said, should not be about 'the transmission and regurgitation of "facts"', an approach he dismissed as only suitable for creating pub quiz contestants. Rather, children should be taught the 'crucial skills of analysis, argument and presentation'.[20]

There it is, the age-old contrast between 'knowledge' and 'skills'. Such contrasts are a stock-in-trade of the progressive thoughtworld but this one, like so many others, is a false dichotomy. Those of us in the reform camp aren't suggesting that children should be forced to memorise facts *in preference to* cultivating their higher-order thinking skills. On the contrary, we value those skills as highly as our opponents do. The difference is, we recognise that children can't be taught these skills without first being asked to memorise a good deal of factual knowledge.

This point was made by Bertrand Russell, the British philosopher, in his essay 'On Education' (1926): 'It is, of course, possible to impart information in ways that do not train the intelligence; it is not only possible, but easy, and frequently done. But I do not believe it is possible to train intelligence without imparting information, or at any rate causing knowledge to be acquired.'[21]

Cognitive Science

Russell's insight has since been borne out by cognitive scientists. Cognitive science has come along in leaps and bounds in the past 30 years and we now have a pretty good understanding of how children develop the capacity for 'analysis, argument and presentation'. The consensus after three decades of research into the development of the human brain is that children cannot engage in critical thinking without having first memorised an array of facts relevant to the task at hand – the approach dismissed as 'rote-learning' by the Cambridge professor of modern history. A child who knows a lot about video games can think critically about video games, but not another subject that he or she knows little about. To imagine that children can learn the 'skill' of critical thinking in one subject and then apply it to another, regardless of how scant their knowledge is of that subject – or to believe that it can be taught as a stand-alone abstract discipline – is simply wrong. Broad comprehension – being able to think critically about a wide range of subjects, as Richard Evans wants children to be able to do – requires a broad base of knowledge. As Aeschylus says, 'Memory is the mother of all wisdom.'

The importance of long-term memory was summed up by three academics in an article for the journal *Educational Psychologist*:

> It is no longer seen as a passive repository of discrete, isolated fragments of information that permit us to repeat what we have learned. Nor is it seen only as a component of human cognitive architecture that has merely peripheral influence on complex cognitive processes such as thinking and problem solving. Rather, long-term memory is now viewed as the central dominant structure of human cognition. Everything we see, hear and think about is

13

critically dependent on and influenced by our long-term memory.[22]

It may sound counter-intuitive, but the approach to teaching that's often characterised as 'Gradgrindian' after the 'eminently practical' schoolmaster in Charles Dickens's *Hard Times* (1854) is, in fact, one of the best ways to switch on a child's brain. We don't need cognitive scientists to tell us this. Writing at the beginning of the nineteenth century, the educational theorist Johann Heinrich Pestalozzi describes the almost magical transformation wrought by getting children to learn things by rote:

> It was at first... merely a parrot-like reproduction of meaningless words. But the sharp separation of individual ideas, the definite order in this separation, together with the fact that the words themselves impressed light and meaning, in the midst of the darkness, indelibly upon their minds, gradually awakened insight into the subject matter, and transformed the darkness into the clear light of day.[23]

Where cognitive science is useful is in explaining how this process works. The reason it's so important to have lots of facts stored in our long-term memory – the reason it's essential if we're to develop the ability to think – is because of the limited space in our working memory.

Typically, we can only hold three or four pieces of new information in our heads at any one time. The moment we focus on another bit of information, we forget one of the others. That would make any form of thinking – even the most rudimentary bit of mental arithmetic – virtually impossible were it not for our ability to retrieve facts from our long-term memory. *While new information quickly overwhelms working memory, a remembered piece of information takes up virtually no space in our working memory*. It's this remarkable property of the human brain than enables us to engage in the sort of problem-solving that professors of education are so keen on. This is why contrasting the learning of facts with these higher-order skills is a false dichotomy; a child cannot develop the latter without having done the former. The idea that you can just jump straight to 'analysis, argument and presentation' and skip the boring bit is at odds with our scientific knowledge of how the brain develops.

Just Google It

Notwithstanding this, some progressives argue that any time spent on getting children to memorise facts is 'pointless' because if they need to retrieve a fact they can just Google it – it's available at 'the click of a mouse', to quote Ian Livingstone.

'Knowing things is hopelessly twentieth century,' says the journalist Justin Webb. 'The reason is that everything you need to know – things you may previously have memorised from books – is (or soon will be) instantly available on a handheld device in your pocket.'[24]

Giles Coren, the restaurant critic of *The Times*, is even more adamant that all book-learning has been rendered redundant by Google:

> What use is any learning at all in an Internet world? What use are books and the ability to read and understand and remember the contents of books when every fact in the world can be on hand in the blink of an eye, literally, right on your Google Glass? What is memory in 2013? What is knowledge?[25]

Let's gloss over the fact that a child without 'the ability to read' wouldn't be able to decipher the information he or she retrieved. The trouble with thinking that Google can play the role of long-term memory is that it underestimates the amount of working memory we use when searching for something on a computer or an iPhone, thereby making it difficult to think at the same time. According to Daisy Christodoulou, author of *Seven Myths about Education* (2013):

> We cannot rely on just looking it up, and we cannot outsource memory to Google. This is because we need those facts in our long-term memory to free up space in our working memory. Looking something up on Google uses up that space in our working memory and means we do not have that space available to process the new information or to combine it with other information.[26]

A second problem with the 'just Google it' approach is that it neglects the amount of foreknowledge a child needs in order to perform an accurate search. The bottom line is you can only find the fact you're looking for in a particular subject if you know quite a lot about that subject already. This was a point made by the journalist and broadcaster Libby Purves:

> Search engines are fallible, despite their spooky air of omniscience: when you really know an obscure subject, you rapidly notice how shallow it is online. And searchers need to have an idea what they are looking for. A great paradox is that the pre-Internet generation may prove to be uniquely privileged, because having learnt facts once makes us diabolically efficient Internet searchers.[27]

Finally, even if a child at the Webb-Coren Academy does manage to perform an accurate search, he or she won't be able to understand the information retrieved without knowing something about the subject already (and that's assuming they've been taught to read). For instance, if you Google 'space station' the Wikipedia entry you pull up is only comprehensible if you already know a bit about 'low Earth orbit', 'propulsion', 'research platforms', etc. The child could perform further searches to plug these gaps, but the same problem will just recur, with him or her being condemned to carry on Googling for ever.

In short, Google is no substitute for committing facts to your long-term memory.

Shift Happens

Defenders of the progressive approach often invoke the rapid advances in information technology, not just search engines, as a reason to dispense with subject knowledge. Another form this argument takes is to claim that knowledge is expanding so quickly in the twenty-first century – and being revised and updated so frequently – that it's pointless to get children to memorise any of it. Instead, they should be taught how to access and evaluate information rapidly. Schools should focus on the *how* of learning rather than the *what*.

This viewpoint is succinctly expressed in a six-minute YouTube video called 'Shift Happens' that trainee teachers are often made to sit through while studying for their education certificates. Among the startling claims made in this video are the following:

According to former Secretary of Education Richard Riley, the top 10 jobs that will be in demand in 2010 didn't exist in 2004.

We are currently preparing students for jobs that don't yet exist... using technologies that haven't yet been invented... in order to solve problems we don't even know are problems yet.

The amount of new technical information is doubling every two years.

For students starting a four-year technical or college degree, this means that… half of what they learn in their first year of study will be outdated by their third year of study.

The implications of these newsflashes are clear. In light of the pace of change in the twenty-first century, it's pointless to teach children subject knowledge, which will soon be redundant. Much better to focus on the 'skills and competencies' that will enable them to seek out and process knowledge themselves. As the Association of Teachers and Lecturers (ATL), one of the largest teaching unions, puts it: 'Rote-learning of facts must give way to nurturing through education of essential transferable skills that enable the next generation to navigate the information age.'[28]

The problem is, what's true of one subject – information technology – isn't true of *every* subject. No matter how many advances we make in the field of computer science, the date of the Great Fire of London will always be 1666. Pythagoras's theorem is as true today as it was in the sixth century BC and Newton's laws of motion, first set out in 1687, still serve to explain the movement of snooker balls. While it's true that subject knowledge is being added to all the time, these advances depend upon mastering what's already known. As Newton said: 'If I have seen further, it is by standing on the shoulders of giants.'

Transferable Skills

Another difficulty with teaching children 'essential transferable skills' instead of subject knowledge is that the skills in question – 'critical thinking', 'problem solving', 'learning 2 learn', etc. – aren't actually transferable. Not only can higher-order thinking skills like analysis and evaluation *not* be taught in isolation from subject knowledge, as cognitive scientists have demonstrated; but once taught they can't then be abstracted from the knowledge they're rooted in and applied to *all* subjects.

A child who has committed enough knowledge of mathematics to his or her long-term memory to be able to solve problems in maths doesn't suddenly become a 'problem solver' in another subject like history. In order to 'detect bias', or 'evaluate sources', or whatever it is the professor of modern history at Cambridge wants children to learn, you first have to acquire a good amount of historical knowledge. Higher-order thinking skills are what cognitive scientists call 'domain specific'. That is, they can only be developed in a particular subject once a student has acquired a sufficient amount of knowledge about that subject. It follows that they can't be transferred from one subject to another. The idea that such skills can be taught *instead of* subject knowledge and then be applied to *all* subjects, regardless of how little children know about them, is nonsense.

To illustrate this point, take Steven Spielberg. He didn't become an expert filmmaker because he learnt how to think critically while studying subjects like French and geography in high school. Rather, he learnt how to be a good director – how to solve problems of composition and exposition – by immersing himself in moviemaking from an early age, starting with his childhood cine camera. In most fields, you need about 10,000 hours of practice to achieve any sort of mastery – to be able to think fluidly and creatively. To assume children can acquire these skills without detailed knowledge of a particular subject is a fundamental misunderstanding about how we learn.

This is the conclusion of Temple University psychology professor Robert W. Weisberg, who has studied a number of creative geniuses, including Thomas Edison, Frank Lloyd-Wright and Picasso. 'You have to immerse yourself in a discipline before you create in that discipline,' he told the *Wall Street Journal*.[29]

Ken Robinson

Okay, say the defenders of the progressive approach. Maybe children *can't* be taught how to think creatively and imaginatively without first immersing themselves in a particular subject. But do they need to be? Surely, children possess these abilities innately? The purpose of a good education should not be to equip children with these higher-order thinking skills, but to nurture the ones they're born with. And the problem with the knowledge-building approach is that it snuffs out these innate talents.

One of the most influential exponents of this view is Ken Robinson – or Sir Kenneth Robinson, to give him his full title. His 18-minute TED talk entitled 'Do Schools Kill Creativity?' is the most-watched TED talk of all time, having been viewed 25 million times. Another of his talks, 'Changing Paradigms', has been viewed over 10 million times on YouTube. Like 'Shift Happens', they're regarded as essential viewing in most university education departments.

Robinson believes that the current system of public education – all over the world – is hidebound by its origins in the Enlightenment and the industrial revolution. He compares schools to factories, accuses them of exhibiting a 'production line mentality' and claims they're designed to prepare children for jobs that no longer exist. They only value one form of intelligence, according to Robinson – academic intelligence, which he defines as a certain type of deductive reasoning and knowledge of the Classics. The pre-eminence of this type of intelligence is the intellectual legacy of the Enlightenment, with its emphasis on rationality. Children not thought to possess this ability are written off, regardless of how talented they might be in non-academic ways. They're dismissed as stupid, when in fact they're 'brilliant'.

This model should be abandoned, he argues, and not just because it's out of date. Children have lots of different abilities so it makes no sense to rank them according to just one narrow definition of intelligence. 'My contention is that all kids have tremendous talents and we squander them – pretty ruthlessly,' he says. He quotes Picasso saying that all children are born artists and gradually have their creativity squeezed out of them as they grow up. 'I believe this passionately. That we don't grow into creativity, we grow out of it. Or rather, we get educated out of it.'

The solution, according to Robinson, is to replace factory-style schools with something more fluid and child-centred. Children should be mixed up together, regardless of their 'date of manufacture', and lessons should be of indeterminate length rather than divided into rigid units of time. He wants to see more 'group learning' – the project work so beloved of Ofsted inspectors – and fewer exams, just like Ian Livingstone. 'We have to rethink the fundamental principles with which we're educating our children,' he says. 'Our task is to educate their whole being...'

Robinson offers two pieces of evidence in support of his thesis. The first is the high incidence of Attention Deficit Hyperactivity Disorder (ADHD) in American schoolchildren. He's sceptical about whether this is a genuine clinical condition – 'It's still a matter of debate,' he says. The real reason millions of children aren't paying attention in class, he thinks, is because they aren't intellectually suited to factory-style schooling.

The second is a longitudinal survey of children designed to test their capacity for 'divergent thinking' at different ages. It turns out that if you ask them to come up with as many 'alternative uses' for paperclips as they can think of, they start out at 'genius level' when they're in nursery school and then become less and less 'creative' as they get older.

Unfortunately, this evidence doesn't stack up. As the cognitive scientist Daniel T. Willingham points out, there are virtually no credible witnesses willing to testify that ADHD is a *malade imaginaire*:

> You'll be hard put to find them at the American Medical Association, the American Academy of Paediatrics, the World Health Organisation, the National Institutes of Health, the Centre for Disease Control, or any of the other national and international organisations that recognise ADHD as a medical condition.[30]

As for the 'alternate uses' for paperclips, of course it's going to be easier for children to come up with novel ideas about what to do with them if they have no idea what they're designed for in the first place. Here's Willingham again:

> Thinking of alternative uses is easier if you are unfamiliar with the typical uses for the object. If you know what a paper clip is, every time you say to yourself, 'Hmm, what might one do with this?' the idea of 'fasten papers!' intrudes.[31]

The most striking thing about Robinson's argument, however, isn't the paucity of evidence. It's his failure to acknowledge that it's all been said before – hundreds of times. He presents his new paradigm as a radical departure from educational orthodoxy, when, in fact, he's expressing a point of view that has been the conventional wisdom in university education departments for at least 100 years.

The same is true of Ian Livingstone. Livingstone describes a typical secondary school as follows: 'You're all required to sit still, working as individuals, no team work, no collaboration, no projects that can be assessed as a group — all doing the same thing.'

Livingstone has four children, but I can only conclude he educated them all privately because you're unlikely to find a single community school that subscribes to this traditional, chalk-and-talk model.

Livingstone wants children to be taught to think critically, but like Ken Robinson he exhibits few signs of critical thought himself. When it comes to the prevailing orthodoxies of the educational establishment, they've accepted them all without a murmur of dissent. You might even say they've learnt them by rote. They criticise 'factory schools' for teaching children how to regurgitate facts, yet in making this very point they are regurgitating progressive dogma.

In fact, the approach they promote as revolutionary – child-centred, emphasis on problem-solving rather than learning facts, collaboration rather than competition, etc. – has been the norm in British and American state schools since the 1970s. It's endorsed by the majority of English school leaders and, until recently, any school departing from this orthodoxy was likely to be punished by Ofsted.[32]

The Romantic Movement

Nearly all of Livingstone and Robinson's ideas – and those of progressive educationalists in general – can be traced back to the Romantic Movement. The Romantics often contrasted the goodness of mankind in its prelapsarian state with the evils of modernity, particularly industrialisation, which was regarded as alien and unnatural. Robinson's belief that children are cramped and hidebound by the artificial constraints of factory-style schooling is a common trope of Romantic literature, from Jean-Jacques Rousseau's *Emile* (1762) onwards. This idea is neatly summed up in the following lines from 'The Schoolboy', one of William Blake's *Songs of Innocence* (1789): 'How can the bird that is born for joy/Sit in a cage and sing?'

Just as most eminently practical men are the prisoners of some dead economist, to quote Keynes, so most progressive educationalists are the prisoners of some dead Romantic poet.

The hostility towards traditional teaching methods displayed by Livingstone and Robinson, which is usually caricatured as whey-faced children being forced to memorise their times tables by a stern schoolmaster standing in front of a blackboard, has its origins in the Romantic movement. Robinson suggests cultivating a child's imagination and creativity, rather than just his or her capacity for logic and reason – what he calls educating 'the whole being' – and seems to think this is a controversial and untested proposal. In fact, this has been at the heart of the progressive approach for over 200 years.

Livingstone rails against exams, which he calls 'random memory tests', and objects to classrooms with children 'all doing the same thing'. This criticism has its roots in the Romantics' veneration of nature. To impose uniform standards on children, to expect them all to do the same thing, is wrong because children are naturally diverse, with different aptitudes and dispositions. It matters not whether they are effective as teaching methods. They are artificial, they go against nature, and that alone is reason enough to condemn them.

Plenty of other Romantic ideas have found their way into the educational mainstream. For instance, the notion that children of nursery school age should spend all their time playing – 'Let kids be kids' – and that trying to teach them anything, such as synthetic phonics or number bonds, is 'developmentally inappropriate'; the view that 'teacher-led' or 'whole class' instruction is inferior to 'child-led' education and that teaching methods should be adapted to the 'individual learning styles' of each child; and, of course, the assertion that 'rote-learning' snuffs out children's creative spark and turns them into unthinking conformists. These aren't unorthodox ideas, as Livingstone and Robinson seem to think. On the contrary, they are almost universally accepted by British and American educationalists. They are the shibboleths of The Blob.

Livingstone and Robinson suggest we should try educating children using a more natural, progressive approach, but this experiment has already been tried. Child-centred learning, an emphasis on providing children with skills rather than knowledge and the downgrading of reason and logic in favour of educating the whole being are the dominant motifs of nearly every state school in Britain and America and have been for at least 25 years.

Even some of Ken Robinson's more 'experimental' suggestions have been tried before – with predictable results. For instance, in 1996 the Walt Disney Company set up The Celebration School in Florida, a monument to numerous 'cutting edge' ideas, including multi-age groupings. Teachers were called 'learning leaders', children were 'learners' and they were taught in 'neighbourhoods' rather than classrooms. Three years later, parents were deserting the school in droves, according to *The New York Times*, fed up with the 'potpourri of progressive methods':

> Parents complained about the lack of homework and the inability to track progress without grades and tests. The unstructured classes confused some parents and students. Teachers struggled with the burdens of multi-age classrooms and working without a written curriculum.[33]

By 2000 most of these 'cutting edge' innovations had been abandoned.

Numerous teachers can testify to just how disastrous these progressive methods have been, not just Christopher McGovern. Many English children acquire neither factual knowledge nor higher-order thinking skills, with roughly a fifth leaving school functionally illiterate and innumerate according to the *Times Educational Supplement*.[34] Those who do well enough in their GCSEs to go on to the Sixth Form are often woefully ignorant about the most rudimentary facts of British life. Here's Daisy Christodoulou again, who's taught English at a number of comprehensives:

> At around the time of the 2010 general election, I spent about half a lesson explaining to a class of 18 year olds – that is, adults who had the vote – the exact role of the monarch in modern Britain. I say monarch – none of them knew what that word meant, or what constitutional meant, which made

attempts to explain a constitutional monarchy difficult. Quite a few were under the impression that the Queen and Gordon Brown – or Gordon Blair, as they'd sometimes say – ran the country together, or that the Queen actually had more power than the Prime Minister. None of them knew who the Chancellor was or what his role was. Most of them could not confidently name one political party.

These were children at an inner-city comprehensive, but even the so-called 'elite' of English schoolchildren, the ones who go on to Russell Group Universities, are scarcely any better informed. Derek Matthews, an economics professor at Cardiff University, was so shocked by the ignorance of British history displayed by his first year economics undergraduates he decided to set them a test. Of his 284 students, only 11.5 per cent could name a nineteenth-century Prime Minister and only 16.5 per cent the British general at Waterloo. Given that these were the top 15 per cent of their age group in terms of educational success, Professor Matthews concluded that the remaining 85 per cent must know even less. 'In other words, we are looking at a whole generation that knows almost nothing about the history of their (or anyone else's) country,' he said.[35]

Matthews' verdict is corroborated by numerous other surveys, such as Lord Ashcroft's (see above p. 9). There's also a substantial body of international evidence showing a decline in the performance of British and American schoolchildren relative to those of other countries.

For instance, in the 2000 Programme for International Student Assessment (PISA), British schoolchildren were ranked 4th in the world for science, 7th for reading and 8th for maths. By 2012, they'd declined to 21st for science, 23rd for reading and 26th for maths. In reading, we are not merely behind our wealthy European neighbours like

Germany and Norway. We're behind Poland and Estonia as well – particularly shocking when you consider that teachers in those countries are paid, on average, less than half what teachers receive in Britain.

America's education system fares even worse. In the 2000 PISA survey, American schoolchildren were ranked 14th for science, 15th for reading and 19th for maths. In 2012, these scores had declined to 28th for science, 24th for reading and 36th for maths. According to a research paper for the peer-reviewed journal *Education Next*, in 2009 America was lagging behind every other OECD country apart from Portugal, Greece, Turkey and Mexico when it came to advanced maths. Six per cent of American schoolchildren were 'advanced' in maths, compared to 28 per cent in Taiwan.[36]

Almost the only thing American schools do really well is teach self-esteem. A 1989 international survey of maths and science skills found that 68 per cent of American high school students thought they were good at maths (the highest percentage of any country), compared to just 23 per cent of South Korean students. Needless to say, in actual tests South Koreans out-perform Americans by a factor of four-to-one.

The countries at the top of the PISA league table are those that still favour the old-fashioned, knowledge-building approach – the teaching method dismissed by progressives as 'drill and kill'. The number one region in the world is Shanghai China, where the child-centred approach is regarded as ludicrously soft. In Singapore, which was 2nd for maths, 3rd for sciences and 3rd for reading in the 2012 PISA table, 80 per cent of 16-year-olds still do O-levels, with papers set by Oxford and Cambridge. It hasn't been possible to take O-levels in England since 1987.

Crystallising Social Differences in Chinese Complexities

Not only has the influence of progressive educationalists placed American and British schoolchildren at a competitive disadvantage on the world stage, it has also increased inequality *within* both countries. One of the great ironies of this debate is that nearly all the advocates of progressive education are on the Left, yet the type of approach they recommend as 'inclusive' and 'equitable' has ended up entrenching poverty and preserving privilege. The reason for this is obvious: If children are learning very little at school, those from under-privileged homes are never going to be able to compete with those from more affluent backgrounds when it comes to securing places at good universities and footholds in lucrative careers. As E.D. Hirsch says, Romantic anti-intellectualism is a luxury of the merchant class that the poor cannot afford. 'The unfairness of an anti-bookish... approach to schooling lies in its assumption that knowledge can be equally withheld from the children of merchants and the children of peasants to achieve the same results,' he writes.[37]

In Britain, the Left's main argument against education reform is that it will increase 'social segregation', seemingly unaware of the contribution that progressive educationalists have made to this state of affairs. Here's Hirsch again:

> Educational progressivism is a sure means for preserving the social status quo, whereas the best practices of educational conservatism are the only means whereby children from disadvantaged homes can secure the knowledge and skills that will enable them to improve their condition.[38]

We don't have to look far to find evidence of the link between The Blob's educational philosophy and inequality. A 2011 report by The Sutton Trust disclosed that the gap in academic attainment between rich children and poor children was higher in Britain than in any other developed country apart from America.[39]

Defenders of the progressive approach dismiss this evidence, claiming that the data is unreliable and, in any case, there are other factors that account for the low PISA scores and increasing segregation of British and American schoolchildren, such as growing income inequality. Dr Alice Sullivan, a lecturer at the Institute of Education, claims the key to raising the attainment of British children is 'redistributive economic policies'.[40] In fact, income inequality is higher in China than it is in Britain or America, yet the poorest 10 per cent of teenagers in Shanghai perform at the same level in PISA maths tests as the richest 20 per cent of teens in Britain and America.[41]

The Left hasn't always been so beholden to The Blob. Until comparatively recently, the orthodoxy among Left-wing intellectuals was that a traditional, knowledge-based education is *an essential prerequisite* of social emancipation rather than an obstacle. Indeed, the notion that ordinary children should be taught useful skills – a view now espoused by the British teaching unions – while only the privileged few should receive a traditional subject-based education, was associated with con-servatives rather than liberals, not least because they were worried that educating working class children properly would threaten the status quo. Take this passage by Robert Tressell from *The Ragged Trousered Philanthropists* (1914), one of the seminal texts of the British labour movement:

What we call civilization – the accumulation of knowledge which has come down to us from our forefathers – is the fruit of thousands of years of human thought and toil. It is not the result of the labour of the ancestors of any separate class of people who exist today, and therefore it is by right the common heritage of all.[42]

That wasn't a piece of high-flown idealism on Tressell's part – it was a view widely shared by ordinary working people. According to Jonathan Rose, author of *The Intellectual Life of the Working Classes* (2001), there was a profound hunger for classical knowledge among the working class in nineteenth-century Britain. His study of borrowing records from Welsh miners' libraries revealed that the most popular books were the 'Great Books' enshrined in the Western canon: Homer's *Odyssey*, Austen's *Pride and Prejudice*, Dickens's *Great Expectations*, etc.[43]

Even Antonio Gramsci, the famous Marxist social theorist, recognised how important it is to teach the workers some factual knowledge if they're to break free of their chains:

The new concept of schooling is in its romantic phase, in which the replacement of 'mechanical' by 'natural' methods has become unhealthily exaggerated.... Previously pupils at least acquired a certain baggage of concrete facts. Now there will no longer be any baggage to put in order.... The most paradoxical aspect of it all is that this new type of school is advocated as being democratic, while in fact it is destined not merely to perpetuate social differences but crystallize them in Chinese complexities.[44]

Gramsci made that observation more than 80 years ago and what seemed like simple common sense to him – that you cannot teach children to think without first providing them with 'concrete facts' – has been borne out by cognitive science. Thanks to our understanding of how the human brain develops, we now know how important it is for schools to focus on the transmission of knowledge. The lessons from this new frontier have been succinctly summarised by Daniel T. Willingham:

> Data from the last thirty years lead to a conclusion that is not scientifically challengeable: thinking well requires knowing facts and that's true not just because you need something to think *about*. The very processes that teachers care about most – critical thinking processes such as reasoning and problem solving – are intimately intertwined with factual knowledge that is stored in long-term memory (not just found in the environment).[45]

A Classical Liberal Education

We know what works: explicit academic goals; a strong focus on subject knowledge; order and discipline in the classroom; and frequent tests to evaluate student performance.

What subject knowledge should be taught? The simple answer is the best and most important work in both the sciences and the humanities – what Matthew Arnold summarised as 'the best which has been thought and said'.[46] This is what's commonly known as a classical liberal education.

And what of the post-modernist challenge? Who is to say what the 'best' or 'most important' knowledge is? Doesn't this involve making contentious value judgements that inevitably favour one ethnic group or social class? This last point was the reason given for rejecting the knowledge-based approach by Martin Johnson, the general secretary of the ATL, in a 2007 interview in the *Guardian*. 'To suggest that some knowledge should be privileged over other knowledge is a bit totalitarian,' he said.[47]

So what can be said in favour of a traditional, subject-based curriculum without sounding 'totalitarian'? When it comes to maths and the sciences – and, by extension, deductive reasoning – the answer is fairly straight-forward. The 'best' and 'most important' simply means those facts and theories that are at present verified by evidence and by our current state of knowledge, and demonstrably exert an influence on our lives and the world around us. The frontiers of knowledge may be advancing all the time, but in the STEM subjects (science, technology, engineering and maths) the fundamentals don't change. As Isaac Asimov points out in his introduction to Carl Boyer's *A History of Mathematics* (1968):

> Once the Greeks had developed the deductive method, they were correct in what they did, correct for all time. Euclid was incomplete and his work has been extended enormously, but it has not had to be corrected. His theorems are, every one of them, valid to this day.[48]

Why teach Darwinism and not Creationism in biology? Because we have good scientific reasons for thinking the Theory of Evolution is true and important. On the other hand, that doesn't mean children shouldn't be taught in their religious studies classes that there are some people who believe in Creationism since that is also a demon-strable and important fact about the world and our society.

The humanities are more controversial. Why teach Charles Dickens and not Naguib Mahfouz or any number of other first-rate authors? Why devote more time to studying the Bible than the Koran? Why prioritise the history of the British Isles or America? For the most part, these are not either/or questions. A classical liberal education shouldn't confine itself to the Western canon, but embrace other cultures and traditions. Nevertheless, the guiding principle should be to teach all children that sub-set of knowledge – and the accompanying vocabulary – that will maximise their chances of leading rich and fulfilling lives. What that sub-set includes will be subject to review, but will always be closely connected to the history and the present nature of the society in which we live, including our international connections. To a great extent, it's what Daniel T. Willingham calls 'taken-for-granted knowledge' – the knowledge that the general reader is assumed to possess by *Times* leader writers, heavyweight political commentators and authors of serious books, and in Britain and America there's no getting around the fact that these authors assume a basic familiarity with the work of 'dead, white European males'.

Defenders of progressive education dismiss the classical liberal approach as 'bourgeois' – or 'inexorably linked with the values of the oppressors and conquerors', as Jo Boaler would have it. Because it is largely confined to Catholic schools, selective state schools and private schools, it is often described as 'elitist'. Not so, as Gramsci pointed out. There's nothing inherently Right-wing or Left-wing about a classical liberal education – it has inspired at least as many Marxist revolutionaries as it has conservative education reformers. And there's little evidence to support the view that teaching 'dead, white European males' is prejudicial to the interests of minorities – that they'll feel excluded or marginalised by having to study Milton, Shakespeare or Chekhov. As the Booker Prize-winning author Howard Jacobson says:

The fear of teaching 'the best' because it is an expression of canonical authoritarianism that will ultimately stultify pupils is rooted neither in reason nor experience; the history of educated man shows that it does the very opposite, equipping the well-taught to disagree, to resist, even to overthrow, from a position of independence and strength.[49]

On the other hand, there's plenty of evidence to suggest progressive teaching methods *do* penalise minorities. Silted as they are with bad educational theories, state schools in Britain and America have become rivers through which existing inequalities flow rather than wellsprings of opportunity. In *The Schools We Need And Why We Don't Have Them* (1996), E.D. Hirsch cites various research studies that show the most decisive influence on a child's educational attainment today is not the school he or she goes to, but the home they're born in. This is in stark contrast to a study conducted in 1925, which showed that poor black children who went to good public schools where they were traditionally taught fared better than well-off white children who attended bad ones.[50]

Advocates of classical liberal education are often accused of being 'elitists' for promoting a form of education that's only suitable for the most able. In fact, that is the position of the progressives who maintain that an academically challenging curriculum is inaccessible to children of average or below-average intelligence – a form of intellectual snobbery flatly contradicted by the research evidence. For example, a study carried out by Adam Gamoran at the University of Leeds shows that the reason America children of below average ability do better at Catholic schools than secular schools is because those in lower sets and streams are taught the same curriculum as those in higher ones. Here's Gamoran's summary of his findings:

In the US, Catholic schools do not exacerbate inequality to the same degree as secular government-funded schools, apparently because they require a more rigorous academic programme in lower-level sets and streams. Further research to explore this finding found two Catholic schools in which students in lower sets made as much progress as those in higher sets. This pattern was attributed to three features: the same teachers taught both high-and low-level classes; teachers held high expectations for low-achieving students, manifested in a refusal to relinquish or dilute the academic curriculum; and teachers made extra efforts to foster oral discourse with low-achieving students.[51]

Further evidence that a knowledge-based curriculum is accessible to mixed ability groups is provided by Massachusetts. In 1993, the state of Massachusetts introduced a content-rich, subject-specific curriculum into its public schools, much like the new English national curriculum that has been dismissed by our own education 'experts' as 'overloaded with facts'.

Needless to say, the gains have been astonishing. The scores of Massachusetts children in the standard tests taken by 10-year-olds and 14-year-olds across America – the National Assessment of Education Progress (NAEP) – shot up and in 2005 Massachusetts children became the first to top the league tables in all four NAEP categories. When the bi-annual tests were repeated in 2007, Massachusetts topped the table again, as it did in 2009, 2011 and 2013.[52]

Not only did *all* children gain as a result of this new curriculum, but the attainment gap between children from different social and ethnic backgrounds narrowed further than in any other state between 1998 and 2005. In addition, between 2002 and 2009 the NAEP scores of African-Americans and Hispanics in Massachusetts improved faster than those of white children, and children from low-income families made similar gains. According to Hirsch: 'If you are a disadvantaged parent with a school-age child, Massachusetts is the state to move to.'

Like Gamoran and Hirsch, I think *all* children should receive a classical liberal education, regardless of background or ability.

This universalist approach, not the progressive method based on 'multiple intelligences' and 'individual learning styles', was the ideal underpinning America's public school system as well as the introduction of comprehensives in Britain in the 1960s and 70s, which the Labour Prime Minister Harold Wilson described as 'grammar schools for all'. The principle that every child should be introduced to the best that's been thought and said, regardless of the circumstances of his or her birth, was the commonly accepted rationale for universal, free education, as summarised by the National Education Association in the 1950s: 'Making freely available the common heritage of human association and human culture opens to every child the opportunity to grow to his full stature.'[53]

If we want all children to grow to their full stature, not just those lucky enough to attend traditional schools, we need to return to this ideal and reject the Romantic gobbledegook – the progressive snake oil – being pedalled by the prisoners of The Blob.

I'll leave you with the words of Robert Tressell, author of *The Ragged Trousered Philanthropists*:

> Every little child that is born into the world, no matter whether he is clever or dull, whether he is physically perfect or lame, or blind; no matter how much he may excel or fall short of his fellows in other respects, in one thing at least he

is their equal – he is one of the heirs of all the ages that have gone before.[54]

Recommended Further Reading

Burkard, Tom, *Inside the Secret Garden* (Buckingham: The University of Buckingham Press, 2007)

Brown, Peter C., McDaniel, Mark A., Reodiger III, Henry L., (eds) *Make It Stick* (Cambridge: Harvard University Press, 2014)

Christodoulou, Daisy, *Seven Myths about Education* (London: The Curriculum Centre, 2013)

Hirsch, E.D., *The Schools We Need And Why We Don't Have Them* (New York: Anchor Books, 1999)

Whelan, Robert, (ed.), *The Corruption of the Curriculum* (London: Civitas, 2007)

Willingham, Daniel T., *Why Don't Students Like School?* (San Francisco: Jossey-Bass, 2009)

Wiseman, Oliver, (ed.), *The Gove Revolution* (London: Standpoint, 2013)

Endnotes

1   In an article for the *Daily Mail*, Michael Gove wrote: 'School
     reformers in the past often complained about what was
     called The Blob – the network of educational gurus in and
     around our universities who praised each others' research,
     sat on committees that drafted politically correct curricula,
     drew gifted young teachers away from their vocation and
     instead directed them towards ideologically driven theory.'
     'I refuse to surrender to the Marxist teachers destroying our
     schools: Education secretary berates "the new enemies of
     promise" for opposing his plans', *Daily Mail*, 23 March 2013

2   George Walden, 'Our education system condemns children
     to second class lives', *Telegraph*, 22 August 2009

3   Chris Woodhead, *Class War* (London: Time Warner, 2003),
     p.110

4   'The dangers of the new National Curriculum', *Telegraph*, 20
     March 2013

5   Richard Evans, 'Make history compulsory for the right
     reasons', *Guardian*, 26 August 2011

6   John White, 'What Schools are For and Why', *Impact No.14*,
     p.7

7   A.V. Kelly, an author frequently included on reading lists
     for PGCE courses, says: '[T]he imposition of any one version
     of knowledge…[is]…a form of social control and… a threat
     to all of the major freedoms identified as essential
     constituents of a free and democratic society.' A.V. Kelly,
     The Curriculum: Theory and Practice (London: Sage, 2009),
     p.41

8   Diane Ravitch, 'Ethnomathematics', *The Wall Street Journal*,
     20 June 2005

9   Margaret Thatcher summed up this common sense approach in her memoirs. 'Though not an historian myself, I had a very clear – and I had naively imagined uncontroversial – idea of what history was. History is an account of what happened in the past. Learning history, therefore, requires knowledge of events. It is impossible to make sense of such events without absorbing sufficient factual information and without being able to place matters in a clear chronological framework.' Margaret Thatcher, *The Downing Street Years* (London: HarperCollins, 1993), p.595

10 Robert Tombs, Letters, *London Review of Books*, Vol.33, No.7, 31 March 2011

11 English at the Crossroads: an Evaluation of English in Primary and Secondary Schools, Ofsted (2009), p.26

12 Chris McGovern, 'The New History Boys', *The Corruption of the Curriculum*, Robert Whelan (ed.) (London: Civitas, 2007), p.71

13 *Ibid*, p.75

14 Robert Peal (writing as Matthew Hunter), 'History Lessons for the 21st Century', *Standpoint*, January/February 2013

15 McGovern, p.61

16 Quoted by William J. Bennett, *Devaluing America: The Fight For Our Culture and Our Children* (New York: Simon and Schuster, 1992), p.43

17 *Ibid*

18 The problem with these approaches isn't that they're completely ineffective – they aren't – but that they're less efficient than more traditional methods. They require teachers to sacrifice time that could be spent talking to children in favour of encouraging children to talk to each other.

[19] Greg Hurst, 'Leave the facts to Google, teachers told', *The Times*, 9 January 2014

[20] Richard J. Evans, 'The Wonderfulness of Us: the Tory Interpretation of History', *London Review of Books*, Vol.33, No.6, 17 March 2011

[21] Bertrand Russell, *The Basic Writings of Bertrand Russell* (London: Routledge Classics, 2009), p.402

[22] P.A. Kirschner, J. Sweller and R.E. Clark, 'Why Minimal Guidance During Instruction Does Not Work: An Analysis of the Failure of Constructivist, Discovery, Problem-Based, Experiential and Inquiry-Based Teaching', *Educational Psychologist* (2006), 41:2, p.76

[23] J.H. Pestalozzi, *Pestalozzi's Educational Writings*, J.A. Green and F.A. Collie (eds) (New York: Longmans, 1912), p.92. Ironically, Pestalozzi is one of the heroes of the progressive pantheon and is responsible for 'object' teaching in mathematics – the wrongheaded notion that the best way for children to learn abstract concepts in maths is by starting with real-world examples.

[24] Justin Webb, 'Learning things is so last century', *The Radio Times*, 13 June 2013

[25] Giles Coren, 'School ruined me and it will ruin my daughter', *The Times*, 7 September 2013

[26] Daisy Christodoulou, *Seven Myths about Education* (London: The Curriculum Centre, 2013)

[27] Libby Purves, 'Learning facts helps us to recognize the truth', *The Times*, 13 January 2014

[28] Association of Teachers and Lecturers, *Subject to Change: New Thinking on the Curriculum* (2007), p.9

[29] Quoted by Joanne Lipman, 'Why Tough Teachers Get Results', *The Wall Street Journal*, 27 September 2013.

According to Lipman: 'Prof. Weisberg analyzed Picasso's 1937 masterpiece Guernica, for instance, which was painted after the Spanish city was bombarded by the Germans. The painting is considered a fresh and original concept, but Prof. Weisberg found instead that it was closely related to several of Picasso's earlier works and drew upon his study of paintings by Goya and then-prevalent Communist Party imagery. The bottom line, Prof. Weisberg told me, is that creativity goes back in many ways to the basics.'

[30] Daniel T. Willingham, 'Is a paradigm shift really needed?', *The Washington Post*, 25 October 2010

[31] *Ibid*

[32] For chapter and verse on how Ofsted inspectors enforce The Blob's ideology, see Daisy Christodoulou, 'Appendix A: Lesson Descriptions from Ofsted reports', *Seven Myths About Education,* (London: The Curriculum Centre, 2013)

[33] Douglas Frantz, 'The Nation: Disney's Brave New Town; Trouble at the Happiest School on Earth', *The New York Times*, 1 August 1999

[34] William Stewart, 'Functionally illiterate and innumerate', *Times Educational Supplement*, 25 September 2010

[35] 'University students "ignorant" of the most basic history facts, study shows', *Telegraph*, 2 July 2009

[36] Paul E. Peterson, Ludger Woessman, Eric A. Hanusheck and Carlos X. Lastra-Anodón, 'Are U.S. students ready to compete?', *Education Next*, Autumn 2011, Vol.11, No.4

[37] E.D. Hirsch, *The Schools We Need And Why We Don't Have Them* (New York: Anchor Books, 1999), p.113

[38] *Ibid*, p.7

[39] Graeme Paton, 'British pupils' social mobility divide is among world's worst', *Telegraph*, 27 November 2011.

[40] Quoted by Graeme Paton, 'State school pupils "failing to take the toughest A-levels"', *Telegraph*, 26 March 2013

[41] Sean Coughlan, 'OECD debunks "myth" that poor will fail at school', *BBC News*, 4 February 2014. The PISA data for Shanghai, China is contentious because the Chinese government prevents children of rural migrants attending mainstream schools in urban areas. However, an analysis of PISA's 2012 results shows no link between an OECD country's ranking in the PISA table and its Gini coefficient. For example, Slovenia's PISA scores are bang on the OECD average, yet it has the lowest Gini coefficient in the OECD.

[42] Robert Tressell, *The Ragged Trousered Philanthropists* (1914) Chapter 1

[43] Jonathan Rose, *The Intellectual Life of the Working Classes* (London: Yale University Press, 2001)

[44] Antonio Gramsci, *Prison Notebooks*, Quaderno XXIX (1932)

[45] Daniel T. Willingham, *Why Don't Students Like School?* (San Francisco: Jossey-Bass, 2009), p.28

[46] Matthew Arnold, *Culture and Anarchy* (1875) Preface

[47] Quoted by Jessica Salter, 'Teachers propose an education department "for silly walks"', *Telegraph*, 30 March 2007. When asked what skills he thought schools should teach children instead of, say, the periodic table, Johnson suggested walking. 'There's a lot to learn about how to walk,' he said. 'If you were going out for a Sunday afternoon stroll you might walk in one way. If you're trying to catch the train you might walk in another way. If you are carrying a pack, there's a technique in that.'

[48] Quoted by Christodoulou. In England, it's doubtful that schoolchildren are learning anything in mathematics, up to and including A-level, that wasn't taught 200 years ago.

49 Howard Jacobson, 'Here's why the "elite" are in charge', *Independent*, 15 May 2010

50 Hirsch, pp.21-22

51 Adam Gamoran, *Standards, Inequality and Ability Grouping in Schools*;
http://www.leeds.ac.uk/educol/documents/163446.pdf

52 'Massachusetts 4th and 8th Graders Lead the Nation in Reading and Mathematics Performance for the Fifth Consecutive Time', Press Release, Massachusetts Department of Elementary and Secondary Education, 7 November 2013

53 Quoted by John Hunter, *The Death of Character: Moral Education in an Age Without Good or Evil* (New York: Basic Books, 2000), p.63

54 Tressell, Chapter 1